Alfred's Premier Piano

Dennis Alexander • Gayle Kowalchyk • E. L. Lancaster • Victoria McArthur • Martha Mier

Alfred's *Premier Piano Course* Performance Book 3 includes motivational music in a variety of styles, reinforcing concepts introduced in the Lesson Book 3.

The pieces in this book correlate page by page with the materials in Lesson Book 3. They should be assigned according to the instructions in the upper right corner of selected pages of this book. They also may be assigned as review material at any time after the student has passed the designated Lesson Book page.

Performance skills and musical understanding are enhanced through *Premier Performer* suggestions. Students will enjoy performing these pieces for family and friends in a formal recital or on special occasions. See the List of Compositions on page 32.

Edited by Morton Manus

Cover Design by Ted Engelbart
Interior Design by Tom Gerou
Illustrations by Jimmy Holder
Music Engraving by Linda Lusk

Copyright © MMVII by Alfred Publishing Co., Inc.
All Rights Reserved. Printed in USA.

ISBN-10: 0-7390-4743-4
ISBN-13: 978-0-7390-4743-9

Use with Alfred's Premier Piano Course,
Lesson Book 3, pages 4–5

Winsome Waltz

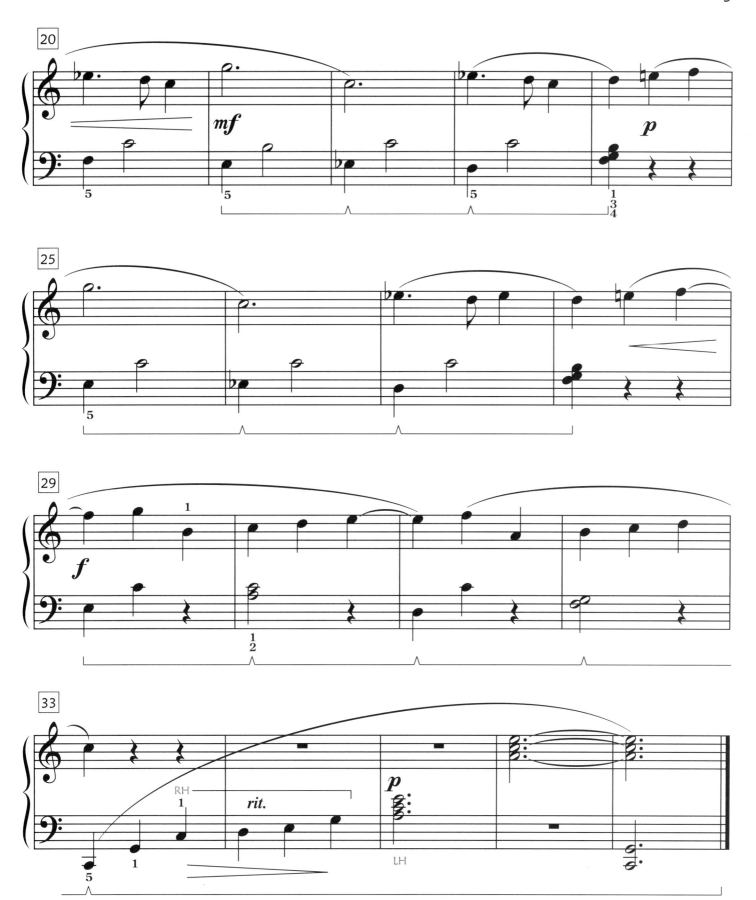

Premier Performer

Move and prepare hands during the quarter rests to help keep a steady tempo.

Antonin Dvořák *(1841–1904) was an important Czech composer, violinist and violist. After success in Europe, Dvořák came to the United States in 1892 and became interested in African-American spirituals and other distinctively American music. In 1893, Dvořák wrote his most famous piece, Symphony No. 9 ("From the New World"), which was influenced by his visit to the Czech-speaking community of Spillville, Iowa.*

New World Symphony Theme

Antonin Dvořák

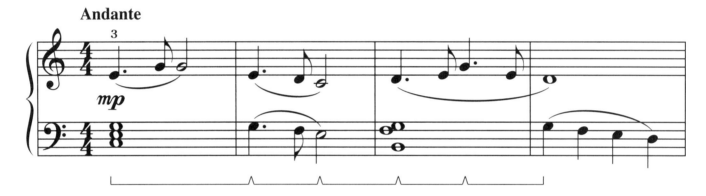

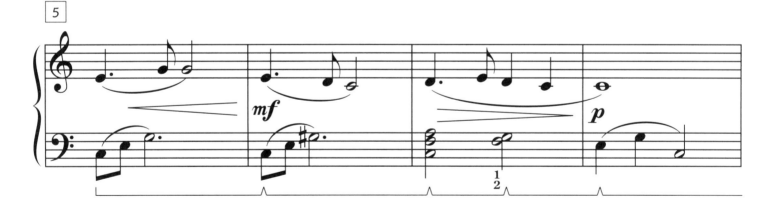

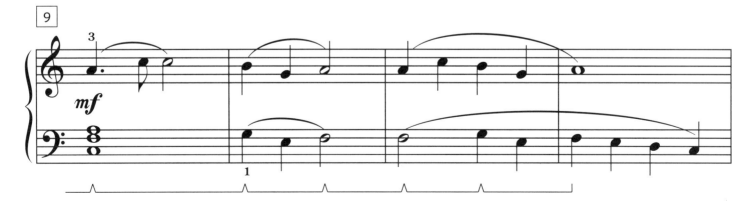

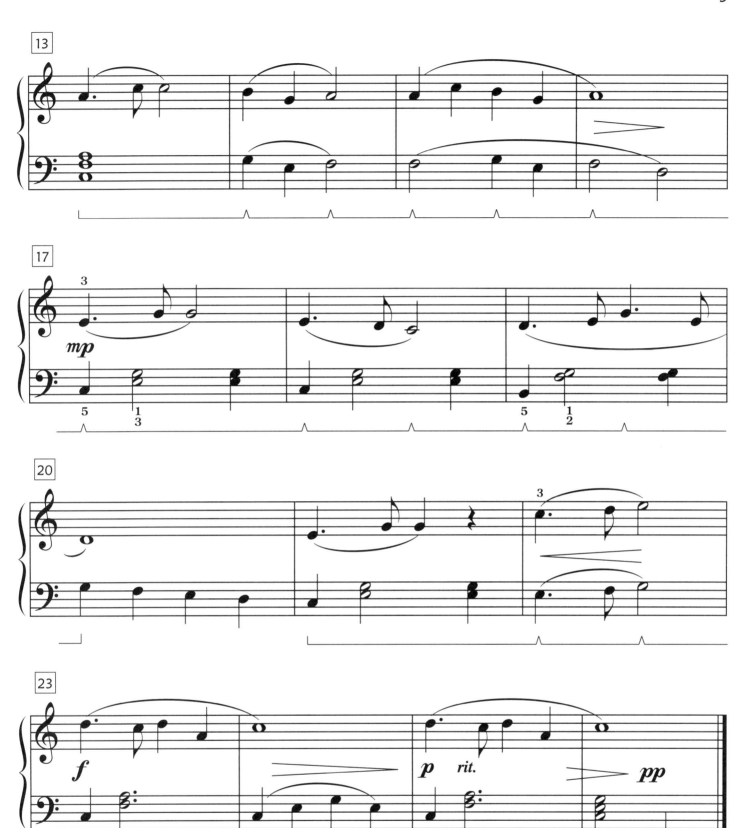

Premier Performer

Play with a gentle, legato sound and listen for a beautiful balance between melody and accompaniment. Listen to play the RH louder than the LH.

6

Math Problem

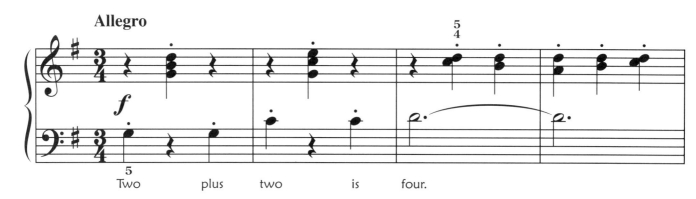

Two plus two is four.

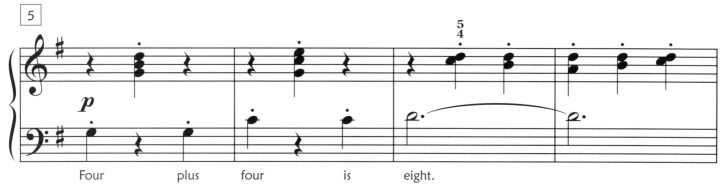

Four plus four is eight.

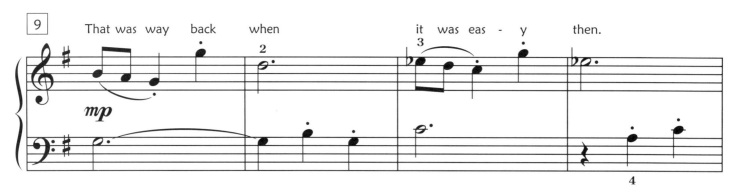

That was way back when it was eas - y then.

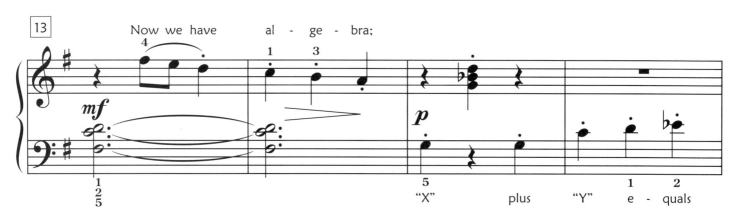

Now we have al - ge - bra;

"X" plus "Y" e - quals

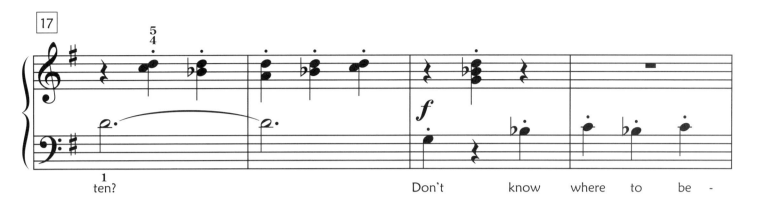

ten?   Don't   know   where   to   be -

gin!

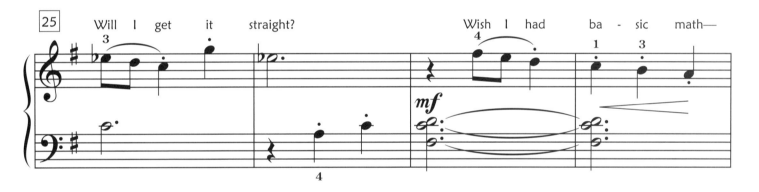

Jazz in the Park

Relaxed waltz tempo

Rhythm Workouts

On your lap, tap each rhythm 3 times daily as you count aloud.

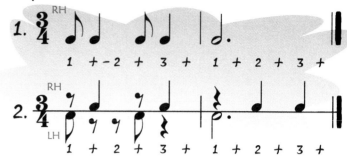

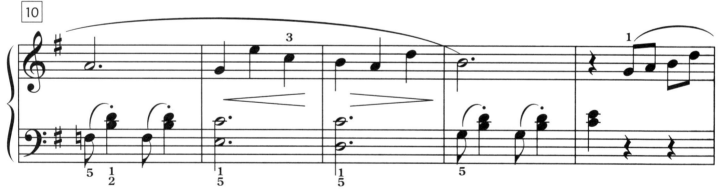

Mississippi Riverboat

Lesson Book: pages 18–19

Moderately, with swing (swing style)

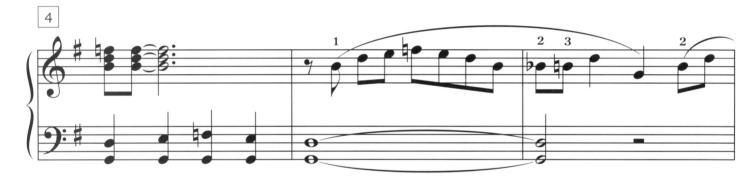

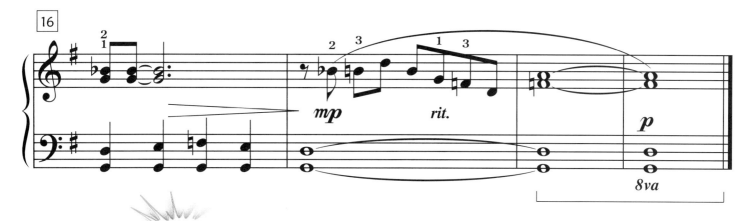

★ **Premier Performer** *Listen for long-short eighth-note patterns in the RH.*

Duet: Student plays as written.

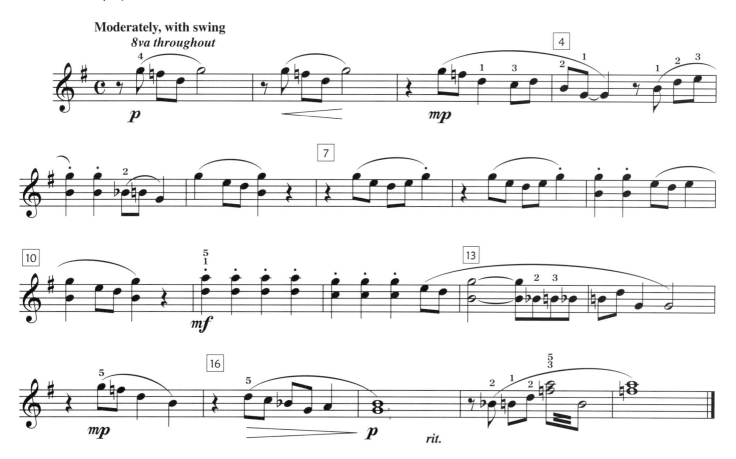

Simple Gifts

Shaker Melody

Duet: Student plays one octave higher.

Thoughts of You

Gently, with expression

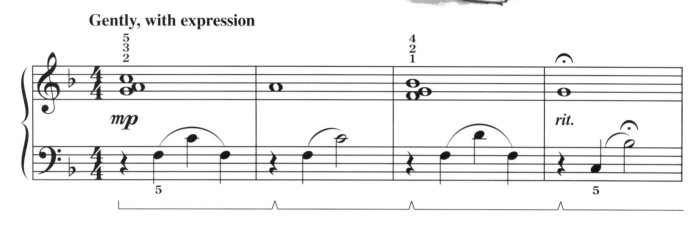

Premier Performer

Play the RH gently with a legato touch throughout Thoughts of You. Listen especially for smooth legato in measures 30–31 when RH 4 crosses over.

Peter Ilyich Tchaikovsky *(1840–1893) was a Russian composer. He began piano lessons at age 5 and soon showed talent as a composer. Many of his highly melodic works were inspired by events in his life. Some of his most notable masterpieces are the ballets* Swan Lake *and* The Nutcracker, *the* 1812 Overture, *the Sixth Symphony ("Pathetique"), as well as two concerti for piano and orchestra, and one concerto for violin and orchestra.* March Slav *was originally composed as a concert march.*

A Cool Caravan

(based on *March Slav*)

Peter Ilyich Tchaikovsky

Premier Performer

Exaggerate the articulations (staccato and legato) in the LH. Play the second note of the LH 2-note slurs with a light thumb.

Lesson Book: pages 32–33

Video Game Challenge

Premier Performer *Exaggerate the accents to create a colorful, dramatic effect.*

Lesson Book: page 35

Handball

Moderately, with bounce

On the school yard, we can play real-ly hard. All we need is a

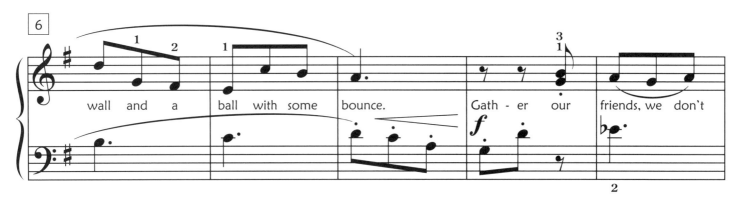

wall and a ball with some bounce. Gath-er our friends, we don't

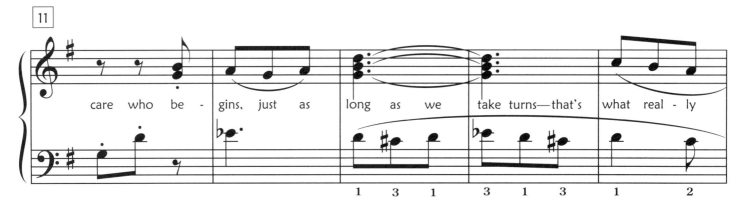

care who be-gins, just as long as we take turns—that's what real-ly

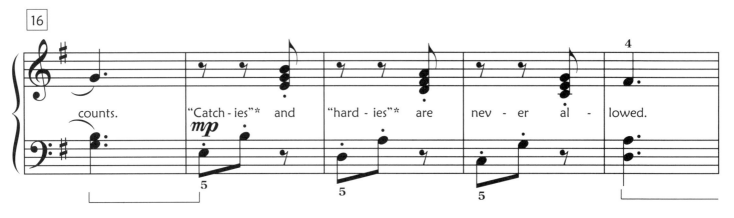

counts. "Catch-ies"* and "hard-ies"* are nev-er al-lowed.

* *Catchie*—catching the ball and throwing it.
  Hardie—hitting the ball too hard.

** *No out of bounds*—the ball can land anywhere and still be in play.
  Slicie—when the ball is hit and travels low to the ground.
  Poppie—when the ball lands exactly at the spot where the wall meets the ground, making a popping sound.

22

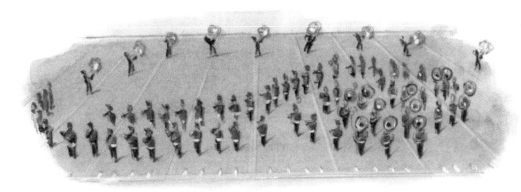

Marching Band Camp

Lively, with determination

Lyrics:
Au - gust is here and that means it's time for Band Camp.
All of my friends wish that they could go for to Band Camp,

Grab all your mu - sic and gear and fol - low me.
when they see me in my brand new u - ni - form.

Premier Performer *Play* Marching Band Camp *with two strong beats per measure (counts 1 and 4).*

24

Starry Night

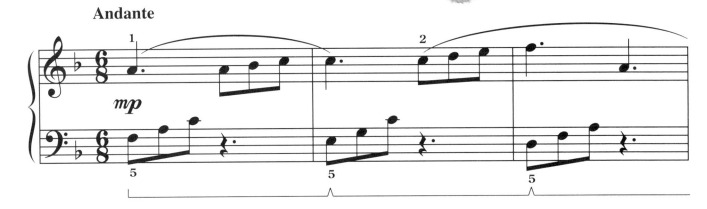
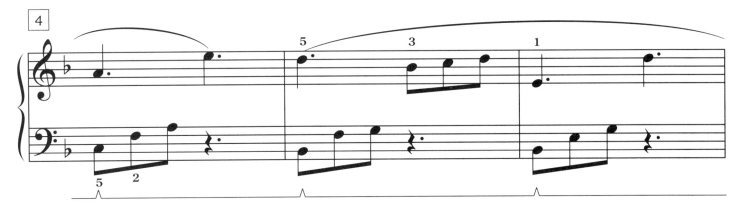
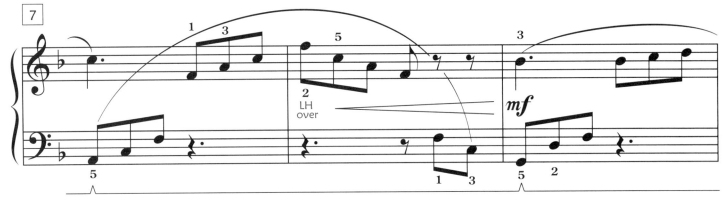
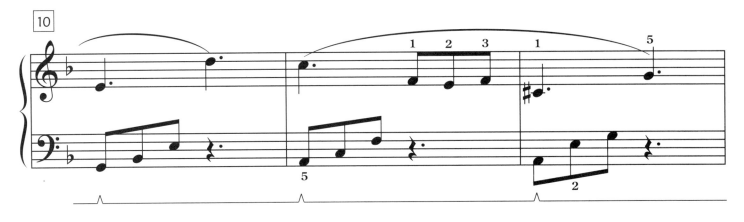

Premier Performer *Listen for clear pedal changes.*

TV Marathon

Moderato

mf On week-end morn-ings, I get up, then on the couch I lay, *ff*

keep my P. J.'s on and stay. I like to watch T - V all

day. I won't go out and play. My fam-i-ly keeps tell-ing me that

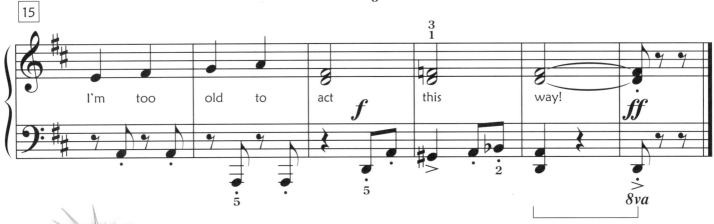

I'm too old to act this way!

Premier Performer *Play the LH louder than the RH in measures 5–8.*

German Dance

Moderately fast

Franz Joseph Haydn

Jean-Joseph Mouret *(1682–1738) was a French composer known for his dramatic works for the stage. Today, the famous Rondeau from his first Suite de Symphonies is well-known as the theme music of the PBS Masterpiece Theater television series.*

Rondeau
(from Suite de Symphonies, No. 1)

Moderate march tempo

Jean-Joseph Mouret

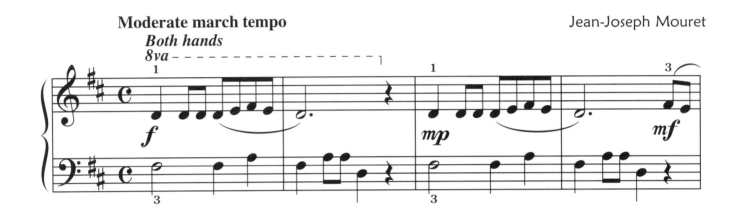

Duet: Student plays one octave higher.

Moderate march tempo

Student LH under RH of duet

poco rit. *8va*

Lesson Book: pages 46–47

Pep Rally

With spirit

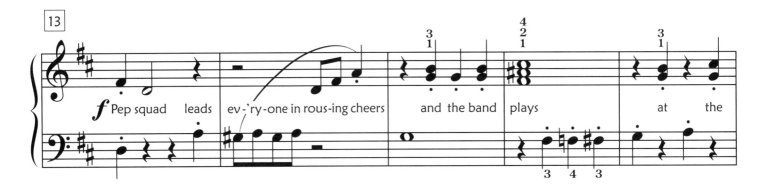

Premier Performer *Listen for a smooth legato sound when the melody passes from the LH to the RH.*

List of Compositions